New England's Arch
by Wallace Nutting

Schiffer Publishing Ltd

4880 Lower Valley Road, Atglen, Pennsylvania 19310

Tina Skinner &
Tammy Ward,
Editors

> *"The city purchaser has not yet come to see the primary law, that nothing is beautiful if unnecessary."*—W. N.

Designed by "Sue"
AdobeJenson /Aldine 721 BT
ISBN: 978-0-7643-2654-7
Printed in China

Published by Schiffer Publishing Ltd.
4880 Lower Valley Road
Atglen, PA 19310
Phone: (610) 593-1777; Fax: (610) 593-2002
E-mail: Info@schifferbooks.com

For the largest selection of fine reference books on this and related subjects, please visit our web site:
www.schifferbooks.com
We are always looking for people to write books on new and related subjects. If you have an idea for a book please contact us at the above address.

This book may be purchased from the publisher.
Include $3.95 for shipping.
Please try your bookstore first.
You may write for a free catalog.

In Europe, Schiffer books are distributed by
Bushwood Books
6 Marksbury Ave.
Kew Gardens
Surrey TW9 4JF England
Phone: 44 (0) 20 8392-8585; Fax: 44 (0) 20 8392-9876
E-mail: info@bushwoodbooks.co.uk
Free postage in the U.K., Europe; air mail at cost.

Contents

Introduction

Among the many careers and titles that have been attached to Wallace Nutting (1861-1941), minister seems the most appropriate as one reads his States Beautiful series. His works are filled with preaching about the appropriate ways to build, furnish, and live in the country, and damnations of those infractions upon good taste and Nature herself.

Nutting left a prolific legacy in his record of images and impressions regarding his native New England states in a series of self-published books. However, he is best remembered today for the furniture he created as well as hand-tinted photography that is coveted by collectors. In *Massachusetts Beautiful* he relates an episode wherein he dumbfounded a local interviewer with his tale about earning a livelihood from apples. In fact, he finally fesses up, he made his living off the images of beautiful blooming apple trees he created, hand tinted, and sold to people in all parts of the country.

Nutting was also successful with a series of books on antiques, mostly detailing furnishings and clocks, and his lectures on the same. He cast himself in a taste-maker role, much as designers have done throughout the ages, offering advice for the proper and most aesthetic appointments for home décor, and urging a lifestyle that evolved around simplicity and the outdoors. Most importantly, he espoused the aesthetic ideal of the late 1600s and early 1700s as an epitome of human accomplishment, and derided the modernization, including the building of much bigger, fancier homes, that he claimed started in the late 1700s.

This book assembles images of the architecture of New England, drawn from six of his publications: *Vermont Beautiful* (1922), *Connecticut Beautiful* (1923), *New Hampshire Beautiful* (1923) *Connecticut Beautiful* (1923), *Massachusetts Beautiful* (1923), and *Maine Beautiful* (1924). Quotations throughout this work draw on Nutting's text and elaborate his position on the best course for America's future development as he preached to an early 20th century nation.

His series of New England books worked so nicely that he expanded into New York, Pennsylvania, and Virginia, and further afield to England and Ireland to produce souvenir books.

Born in Rockbottom, Massachusetts, Nutting spent twelve of his childhood years in Maine. His education gave him wide exposure to the New England states, as his studies included time at Phillips Exeter Academy (New Hampshire), Hartford Theological Seminary (Connecticut), and Harvard University (Massachusetts) from where he graduated in 1887.

A year later he married Mariet Griswold, of Buckland, Massachusetts. Though they had no children, if the imperial "we" he often refers to in his books is to believed, Mrs. Nutting worked in partnership with him on many home restorations, as well as the leisurely explorations of the New England states. "Having spent some years in each one of the New England States the author feels at home in all of them," Nutting wrote in *Massachusetts Beautiful*.

These explorations could only have been so leisurely, however, when one looks at the volume of Nutting's work, including the release of books about four of the states in one year alone. Wallace stated in his forward to *New Hampshire Beautiful* that he "made all the pictures himself and has written the bulk of the text," though he included poems by several other writers as credited.

Nutting died at his home in Framingham, Massachusetts on Saturday, July 19, 1941, at age 79. He left a legacy of antiques and ephemera sought after by collectors today. This book pays tribute to Nutting's eye for architecture. The text explores his antiquarian's insistence that the early 1700s represented the finest achievements in home construction, situation, and appointments, and an insistence that change and the whims of fashion would only serve to sully that legacy.

> *"In this series of books we are always thinking of the dweller on the soil, and the villager who looks out on the same fair landscape that has filled the eye of his fathers at least to the third and fourth generations."* —W. N.

Pastoral Paradise

How To Select a Farm Place

In Massachusetts Beautiful, Nutting offered the following advice for readers contemplating a move to the country. He labeled those who remained in a city insane. His advice follows, only slightly abbreviated.

1st. Do not despise small buildings. It is easy to spend and sometimes one begins too large. A little cottage doubled is far more artistic than a big square house.

2nd. Avoid clay soil for your residence. It is damp most of the year and the cellar is always so. Seek clay soils for at least a portion of your land. Clay is the foundation of agriculture. Soils are divided into clay, clay loam (three-quarters clay, one-quarter sand), loam (half and half), sandy loam (three-quarters sand, one-quarter clay), and sand.

3rd. Avoid rocky fields. It never pays to clear stones. It takes generations and then they are not cleared. Such fields may be turned into pastures if there is a moderate amount left of easily arable soil. Occasional small stones do not harm, but ledgy fields or fields with numerous small stones are vexing and profitless.

4th. In ledgy or stony ground an orchard may be set, as such soil is often well fitted for fruit and sheep. Sheep may be turned to graze in this pasture if the trees are protected by wires.

5th. Find a country place with possible spring sources to feed the house, by gravity. This is highly desirable, as constant pumping even by machinery is a perpetual nuisance and expense.

6th. Seek first for a farm off the road, approached by its own little side road.

7th. Avoid buildings where the barns are so placed as to interfere with the outlook. If barns or out buildings are very numerous it is far better to remove the poorer ones. There are almost always too many and the upkeep of many buildings is very expensive.

8th. The intimate view is more important than the distant view. If an elevation means wind and bareness it is better avoided. The ideal location is a high slope, not too steep, and one that is sufficiently wooded.

9th. Bury your telephone wires or bring them in from the rear. It is almost better not to live in the country if there are to be poles in your road.

10th. A tractor capable of cutting the old wood around the farm, as well as ploughing and hauling, is now of the first importance, and will save its coast several times over in short time.

11th. Do not go into any kind of farming that leaves you stranded in the case of failure of help. A farmer can himself feed a number of sheep and young stock, but if he has more than two cows his labors become onerous in case his farm hands desert him.

12th. Make all arrangements so that you will be as independent as possible of outside connections of men, animals, machines or power.

13th. Farm lands should contain fields, pastures and woodland, whatever else they may lack. Good orchards can seldom be bought. A wood lot is important for the sense of independence it gives, for its esthetic advantage, and also and perhaps principally as an investment.

14th. Do not bother to drain swampy lands unless the soil is imperatively required. Coarse grass has its uses, and in a dry season is often a resource.

15th. Small fruits carefully attended are a pretty sure source of some profit. High bush berries should not be neglected.

16th. Not more than one horse should be kept on a farm and that number is often one too many. Horses are the most expensive features of the farm. If a horse is to be kept it should be for the love of it only, or for a few rough odd jobs.

17th. Do not be misled by the notion that artificial manures are sufficient. Absolutely necessary humus must be supplied from the barnyard or through the ploughing under of nitrogen crops.

18th. Do not fall into the error of building a lot of fences. The cost is vast and the advantage is often nil. Nothing but the pasture should be fenced.

19th. When installing plumbing, pay no attention to the statements of the plumber that it won't freeze. Let no pipes run up from the outside walls or anywhere near them.

20th. The drainage about the farm buildings aside from the sewer should be natural.

21st. In obtaining a country place inevitable disappointment will follow if financial profit was the first consideration, because no man will make enough to satisfy him. The first and last and constant feeling should be the joy in the occupations connected with developing and carrying on the farm place.

The old Wallace Nutting homestead, Connecticut.

The Wallingford homestead, Connecticut.

A home located on Dover Street in the Portsmouth area.

"We have always had a fondness for seeing the old walls and homesteads set on the slopes of the mountains." —W. N.

A rural scene in Massachusetts.

The Mission House in Stockbridge, Massachusetts.

The Abbot house in Andover, Massachusetts.

A home in Framingham, Massachusetts.

This Massachusetts home was built in 1700.

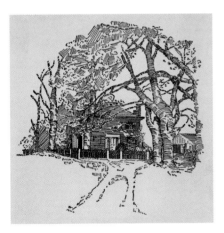

A homestead on the Naugatuck, Connecticut.

An inhabited cove in Newcastle, New Hampshire.

Benning Wentworth's home in Newcastle, New Hampshire.

The Balch house, before restoration, in Beverly, Massachusetts.

Whittler's home, near Amesbury, Massachusetts.

A home on the Concord-Acton Road in Massachusetts.

A home in the hills of Vermont.

A farm nestled in the gently rolling hills of Vermont.

Beautiful Homes

In his selection of home, Wallace Nutting very clearly, and adamantly, preferred those of a hundred and fifty years earlier. "It is not worth while to enter upon the description of the less worthy dwellings of the waning period 1780 and onward," he wrote. "It was a time of large and well built dwellings so far as the carpentry was concerned, but the lower roofs, the absence of cornices, the disappearance of good porches, and various other declinations of style such as inferior mantels, incline us to direct our attention more particularly to the earlier time."

Perhaps his most telling note, in *New Hampshire Beautiful*, is all the summary necessary: "The newest house in New Hampshire is not worth mentioning."

"Nature has yet to be unveiled. Like a rural maiden whose perfections the world does not know, there are landscapes, bowers, dells, becks and burns, there are brows and bosoms of nobility and purity awaiting the awakening of men of spirit and of fire, who have in them poetry and taste, the knowledge of the beautiful and the passion to record what they so passionately see."—W. N.

A residence on High Street in Wiscasset, Vermont.

An old home in Richmond, Maine.

Standish dwellings, Maine.

Residences located on a street in Union, Maine.

VINE CORNICE, NEW VINEYARD

Vine cornice, New Vineyard, Maine.

Home and barn in Vermont.

A Sheepscot cottage, Maine.

A cottage in Randolph, Maine.

Garrison House in York, Maine, was built about 1645.

The Tristran Perkins house, Maine.

> *"People will do what is fashionable. We follow trends, and caught in such a trend it is almost impossible to escape it. If only a trend toward permanent structures can be started, the greatest material benefit to America will result."*—W. N.

A country cottage in Washington, Maine.

A Dresden, Maine, retreat.

A Readfield, Maine, homestead.

The Cooper-Austin House in Cambridge, Massachusetts.

Adams House in Quincy, Massachusetts.

Sir William Pepperell House in Kittery, Maine.

River Knoll Farm in Maine.

A residence in Wiscasset, Maine.

Wiscasset, Maine, Mansion.

A quaint overhang on Portland-Standish Road, Maine.

Jason Russell house in Arlington, Massachusetts.

A home in Concord, Massschusetts.

A Weston, Massachusetts, Homestead.

The Manning House in Billerica, Massachusetts.

A home in Weston, Massachusetts.

23

The Block-House in North Edgecomb, Maine.

"A garden is an extension of the dwelling, a kind of sacred spot out of doors into which no evil thought should come and only beauty and repose find place."

A Pembroke, Massachusetts, house and garden.

The house and gardens at Pittsfield, Massachusetts.

Woolwich, Maine, Homestead.

The Short house in Newbury, Massachusetts.

Weymouth, Massachusetts, Homestead.

General Lincoln House in Hingham, Massachusetts.

The Fairbanks homestead in Dedham, Massachusetts.

A Middlesex, Massachusetts, lean-to.

Hollyhock Row in Haverhill, Massachusetts.

A residence on Hamilton-Wenham Road, Massachusetts.

The Eleazer Arnold house, Massachusetts.

"A home in the mountains ought to blend in its aspect with its surroundings and be of a character suggesting sturdiness, permanence and the beautify of its environment."—W. N.

Old Manse, Concord.

29

King Hooper house in Danvers, Massachusetts.

Buckman Tavern in Lexington, Massachusetts. "The town has recently bought and to some degree restored the Buckman Tavern, an instance of very fine public spirit as the cost was great."

Saugus overhang house, Massachusetts.

Coffin House, Massachusetts.

Topsfield, Massachusetts, homestead.

A home in Quincy, Massachusetts.

A colonial roof in Massachusetts.

A homestead in Shrewsbury, Massachusetts.

An old home in Norfolk, Massachusetts.

Fashionable 'Sconset, Massachusetts.

A Gambrel corner, Massachusetts.

A nook in Plymouth, Massachusetts.

A Hyannis byway.

> *"A garden enclosed has been the delight of all ages and nearly all races of men. Its secluded beauty open only to heaven is an image of an ideal human soul open to upper influences, but shut off in its more sacred aspects from the world."*

**A home and large garden
in Connecticut.**

A residence in Hingham, Massachusetts.

A village mansion in Northampton, Massachusetts.

The Thatcher cottage in Yarmouthport, Massachusetts.

The Stearns house in Bedford, Massachusetts.

A modest two story home
in Massachusetts.

37

Sandwich, Cape Cod.

A very picturesque barn in Connecticut.

A vine covered entryway of the Pierce-Little home in Old Newbury, Massachusetts.

Wright tavern in Concord.

The Winslow house in Marshfield, Massachusetts.

A glimpse of Nantucket charm.

The John Alden house located in Duxbury, Massachusetts.

The Major Bradford home in Jones River, Massachusetts.

"When a great body of men of various callings become enthused by the idea of permanent edifices, stone work will grow popular and easy to secure. We look forward to a complete change in American homes within a hundred years. By that time, if we are to endure, we shall cover our country with beautiful structures built of stone and built on stone."—W. N.

A home in Framingham, Massachusetts.

The Hancock-Clarke house in Lexington.

The Cowan house in Concord.

The Dwight-Blaney house, in Massachusetts.

The Craddock mansion in Medford, Massachusetts.

A three-storey home in Nantucket.

The Fairbanks house in Massachusetts.

An early Georgian home in Suffield, Connecticut.

A residence in Withersfield, Connecticut.

A homestead in North Andover, Massachusetts.

An early Georgian home in Suffield, Connecticut.

A stately old home in Middletown, Connecticut.

Hospitality Hall in Wethersfield, Connecticut.

A home located in New Haven County, Connecticut.

A Mansard of 1787 in Connecticut.

A 17th century home in Farmington, Connecticut.

Brookfield Hall in Connecticut.

A home in Wethersfield, Connecticut.

A Suffield Homestead.

Another Wethersfield residence.

The Curtis residence in Stratford, Connecticut.

A cozy Connecticut home.

A residence in East Haddam, Connecticut.

A charming small home in Connecticut.

A hillside home in Connecticut.

A Salem Gambrel in Connecticut.

A homestead in Mystic, Connecticut.

A dwelling with an overhang in Colchester, Connecticut.

This Dutch cottage is located in North Haven, Connecticut.

An overhang house in Farmington, Connecticut.

A house on New Britain-Hartford Road in Connecticut.

A residence in Talcottville, Connecticut. Note the chimney on each corner.

An old stone house in Guilford, Connecticut.

"The dwellings in New Hampshire average very markedly large. We cannot attribute this wholly to the almost universal boarding-house habit which has transformed many a farm-house into a twenty-room edifice."—W. N.

A gable home in Groton, Connecticut.

A homestead in Simsbury, Connecticut.

"The best place to find a quaint old house for restoration is on any road at distances of not more than five miles apart. This sentence may be execrable grammar, but it tells the truth."—W. N.

The Thomas Lee House in East Lyme, Connecticut.

The Wolcott Homestead in Litchfield, Connecticut.

56

A Stratford, Connecticut, hewn overhang.

The old Huguenot house in New London, Connecticut, "a relic of earlier times. Its excellent stone end, of which the chimney is only a projection is further enhanced in attractiveness by vine growth. Happily, the little picket fence has been retained around the front."

The first house on Daniel Webster Road in New Hampshire.

The Old Parsonage, Westmoreland, New Hampshire.

A home in Madison, Connecticut.

The Jackson House, built circa 1660 is considered the oldest dwelling in Portsmouth. "The Jackson house … has a good many merits of a typical character, and … we are of the opinion that almost any house anterior to 1700 is worth preserving…. The author has sometimes been tempted to purchase and restore this house but he thinks he has done more than his duty in such restorations."

The birthplace of Daniel Webster located in Franklin, New Hampshire.

The Warner house in Portsmouth, New Hampshire. "The Warner mansion," Nutting wrote, "is thought by most to be one of the first, as it is perhaps the finest, of early examples of the gambrel roof."

The house of the seven gables, Massachusetts.

The old post office in Durham, Connecticut, was singled out by Nutting as the perfect example of the overhang style of architecture, and "very remarkable as a continuation of the earliest American style."

Cape Cod Cottages

In Massachusett's Beautiful, Nutting both explains the origins of the humble cottage, and insists upon its continuance in the vernacular:

"The Cape Cod cottage has achieved the distinction of receiving this specific name. There are many thousands of houses of precisely the same type scattered through New England, but this cottage is so uniformly found at the Cape that we take no issue with the appellation. The stranger at Cape Cod is often puzzled by the term "double house." In the Cape Cod significance, this phrase refers to a house with a chimney in the middle and a room on both sides. Frequently the space on either side of the chimney is divided into more than one room... The name arose on Cape Cod from the fact that the first settler built a tiny house with the chimney at one end and perhaps a front and rear room downstairs, the rear room being a small bedroom opening off the kitchen. This is called a 'single house.'

"... these houses are almost always shingled. Where they are left unpainted, as is usually the case, they acquire a beautiful gray, which cannot be distinguished from the stone walls found before one reaches the Cape where such houses also appear. This gray effect is the result of intimacy with the weather and requires some years to reach its perfection. In many instances white paint has been applied to these houses and never with aesthetic advantage. The dweller within the cottage may indeed protect his dwelling and feel that he has a trimmer anchorage with a painted house, but he loses that mellow melting into the atmosphere , and that nameless charm of roof and side wall in the same natural tint.

"No possible preparation of the shingle can give an artificial color matching this superb gray. Furthermore, the side wall of a house will last for generations without paint... Of course, the old shingles were often made of shaved pine, which render them almost eternal.

A Cape Cod cottage and mill.

Windows and Doorways

A bow window overlooking a garden in Massachusetts.

A sunroom extension for a home in Manchester, Vermont.

An entryway into a home in Durham, New Hampshire.

A photo inspired a line drawing of this picturesque entryway to a summer
home in the Monadnock region of New Hampshire.

The entryways are shown to two homes in the Chocorua mountain region of New Hampshire, noted as the Richter and Warren homes. "The Richter door is an interesting example of the iron post and chain style in connection with the front steps and the fence, and is quite typical. The relieving arches over the windows are also excellent."

The Syringa door located in Chester, New Hampshire.

The entryway to Langdon's home in Portsmouth, New Hampshire.

Two more illustrations of entryways of Portsmouth homes.

Another entryway into a Portsmouth home. "We have somewhat largely illustrated the doorways and dwellings of Portsmouth, partly because at one time we rescued the Wentworth-Gardner house in that city from degradation, and therefore spent very much time in the city, and partly because of the inherent attractiveness of the place."

This entryway has an arch within an arch, located in Portsmouth.

One more entryway among Portsmouth's collection of beauties.

A home and garden in Chester, New Hampshire.

Walkway leading up to the entry of a Hancock home in New Hampshire.

An entryway in a Wethersfield home, Connecticut.

A covered entryway, Connecticut.

A home in Connecticut.

An opened doorway on a Litchfield, Connecticut, home.

A Cos Cob, Connecticut, door.

71

A covered doorway on a Hampton, Connecticut, home.

Steps leading up to a back entry in Connecticut.

72

A covered porch in Litch-
field, Connecticut, is a portion of the famous old Walcott
mansion.

A residence in Litchfield,
Connecticut.

A covered double-door entryway in Connecticut.

A covered entry to a Brookfield home, Connecticut.

A home in Salem, Massachusetts.

A home in Nantucket, Massachusetts.

The Duxbury homestead, Massachusetts.

Two women share news before a home in Nantucket.

A home in Nantucket.

A lovely Brookfield, Massachusetts, door.

Blossom covered entryway in Massachusetts.

A Quincy, Massachusetts, door.

The Mission door, Stockbridge, Massachusetts.

"The back doors of old houses are more interesting than the front doors, especially when the dry stone wall supplied a foundation for the steps, and flowers and vines and trees completed the setting. Little paradises are often feasible at back doors.... An old back door has more of humanity in it than any other part of the homestead."

A Braintree, Massachuesetts, old timer.

The Mitchell door in Nantucket.

The White Door, Salem, Massachusetts.

"There is ever a kind of coquettishness about an old house. It beckons us to know what hidden charms it contains."—W. N.

A Scituate, Massachusetts, door.

A South Shore, Massachusetts, door.

A Hatfield, Massachusetts, door.

An entryway in Vermont.

The front door of the Sparhawk House in Kittery, Maine.

82

Entryway in Vermont.

83

A vine covered entryway in Vermont.

A side entrance in Vermont.

Interiors

Wallace Nutting shares the following parable in *New Hampshire Beautiful*:

"We remember a gentleman of wealth bought a beautiful old house. The deciding factor which induced his purchase was the charm of the home room. Under the auspices of his better half this room was again furnished, but – with Victorian stuff. The result was that the room wholly lost its charm and no one went into ecstasies over it.

"The room required furniture of the Revolutionary period, like simple Windsor chairs, large braided rugs, early American prints (not the Currier & Ives period), an occasional silhouette, an ancient map and, for the rest of the furniture, bandy-legged tables and a desk of the same style, with an early Windsor settee or a settle and an early American clock. A couple of tavern tables would have constituted all the necessary objects to add. Of course, a baby chair or two always gives a touch of interest to such a room. One or two candle stands and a sconce of a simple sort could be used."

In elaborating upon appropriate furnishings for an historic home, he writes that "the errors in furnishing such a room are in the direction of elaborateness, of incongruity... The one modern over-stuffed chair is sneaked in, to make the room attractive for John, as the wife explains. The ruin is complete. She does not know that a rush seated chair is the most comfortable ever made, besides being durable and cleanly. How long can an overstuffed chair be used with decency? Possibly a week. Almost invariably such chairs are unclean, always unsanitary, and in bad taste....

"There is no possible excuse on the score of comfort, taste, durability or expense in using new and old together. If one insists on new furniture it should be closely copied from the old, but without an effort to pass it off for old. We have known not a few who really wished to be deceived and never turned a hand to ascertain the facts. The last error in furnishing is to crowd too much into a room. The walls particularly are rendered hideous by a large number of little sketches, run up and down in diagonals, or like the picture page of a Sunday supplement, whereas charm is secured only by a very few pictures, kept well apart. The floors are spoiled by a great assortment of little rugs... So the floor is made to look like a large number of griddle cakes on a quick lunch window gas stove.

"There must be far more open space than furniture.... People cling to their horrible furniture almost as passionately as to their pet sins."

The Warner door on a house in Portsmouth.

A hall bench in Connecticut.

A home in Andover, Massachusetts.

Inside a central hall in Connecticut.

A high ceiling living room with wood floors located in Portsmouth.

An early Victorian living room in Hancock, New Hampshire.

The city of Paris is papered onto this wall in a Chocorua, New Hampshire, home.

The high sea with large ships is the backdrop for this Georgian room in the Gardner home, New Hampshire.

The parlor in the Warner home in Portsmouth.

> *"Our love for quaintness and simplicity should lead, as we believe, to the rejuvenescence of the gambrel roof in the one story variety. Such a dwelling, with a small kitchen built with a wing, and with the same gambrel and without dormers, affords good windows on the gable end and six large rooms which is enough for the average modern family. In fact that family, if it goes on at its present rate of diminution, will get on well with the one room house of the first settlers."*—W. N.

A tranquil parlor scene in Connecticut.

The living room of a home in Southbury, Connecticut.

A living room in a home located in Wethersfield, Connecticut.

Living room in a Wethersfield, Connecticut, home.

A parlor in Massachusetts labeled "the height of luxury."

This living room in Connecticut has exposed beams overhead.

The Yorktown Parlor located in the Webb House in Wethersfield, Connecticut.

The parlor of a 1752 home in Connecticut, decorated with pastoral scenes.

A huge fireplace in a Saugus home, Massachusetts.

Life in the country is portrayed on the walls of this parlor in Connecticut.

Quilt making in a Newburyport, Massachusetts, home.

An old drawing room in Massachusetts.

A parlor in Massachusetts.

A kitchen scene in Connecticut.

Large kitchen and fireplace in Connecticut.

A North Shore, Massachusetts, kitchen.

Abraham Browne house kitchen, Massachusetts.

The Goulding House kitchen in Sudbury, Massachusetts.

The Coffin House kitchen in Massachusetts.

Corner Cupboards

"Corner Cupboards and side cupboards are admirable, and with a fireplace almost make a dining room. To be sure, in the old days, the corner cupboard was more often in the parlor, but if we go back far enough we shall find that the parlor was the dining room. And when another room was reserved for dining the cupboard was left in the parlor, partly that callers might see the treasures therein." —W. N.

A corner cupboard that was built into a Connecticut home in 1730.

A built in china cabinet in Connecticut.

99

A shell cupboard in Connecticut.

A Groton cupboard in Connecticut.

An old bedchamber in a Suffield, Connecticut, home.

100

Two bedrooms in the Webb house of Connecticut.

Two views of another bedroom in the Webb House.

A fireplace warms a Concord bedroom.

**Bedrooms in the Quincy homestead in
Newburyport, Massachusetts.**

Stairways and Halls

This staircase is in the Pierce House in Portsmouth.

The entry hall of the Gardner
house in Portsmouth.

A Woodbury, Connecticut, home
with a small view of the staircase.

A Groton, Connecticut, stairway.

A glimpse inside of a home built in 1730 in Connecticut.

Goulding Hall in Massachusetts.

The Jaffrey House hall in
Massachusetts.

THE SPARHAWK HOUSE HALL, KITTERY

The Sparhawk House hall in
Kittery, Maine.

Fireplaces

In Connecticut any house dated before 1820 had large chimneys. Before 1740 chimneys were often, if not generally, of stone. There was always a fireplace in every principal room downstairs; and we remember no instance in which a large chamber failed of having a fireplace. The larger the fireplace, broadly speaking, the older the house. The kitchen fireplace was the largest, and the chamber fireplaces were quite small, even in the earliest period."

"In such a room, the fireplace is the central feature. It should always be of good size, though not necessarily huge. Anything less than five feet wide is a little scant. The top should not be arched but straight, with an iron to support the brick, unless the fireplace is of stone.

"A crane with a tea kettle, a small pot with its hook, a warming pan, a toaster on the hearth, an old fashioned fire shovel and tongs complete the equipment.... A little fire should always be smoldering here, except during the summer heat.

This mantle is located in a large Portsmouth home.

108

The Gardner house, New Hampshire.

**Fireplace in the Pierce House,
New Hampshire.**

109

Living room of a home in Portsmouth.

> *"...we are almost ready to say that bad architecture is immoral."* —W. N.

A chimney nook in a Connecticut home.

A large fireplace keeps the babies warm in Connecticut.

A dining room in a New Haven county home.

Hamilton Holt kitchen in Woodstock, Connecticut.

An old mantel in Connecticut.

A fireplace warms a bedroom in
Sheraton, Connecticut.

A late 18th century fireplace
in Connecticut.

113

A Groton, Connecticut, fireplace.

"How can an intelligent man worship God honestly in an edifice with wooden, hollow, sanded, imitation Gothic buttresses. You can keep the worshipers in such an edifice honest only by keeping them ignorant."—W. N.

A parlor in Massachusetts.

A Concord, Massachusetts, historical society room.

A room in the old Danvers home, Massachusetts.

Dining room of a home in Framingham, Massachusetts.

A fireplace sketched from a Connecticut home.

The dining room at the Quincy house, Massachusetts.

Quilt making at the Quincy homestead, Massachusetts.

Stockings dry over a fire in Massachusetts.

A mother and babe in Connecticut.

A parlor fireplace in Massachusetts.

A fireplace in the parlor of Josiah
Griswold, Massachusetts.

Floral arrangement before the fire in Massachusetts.

A parlor of 1800, still functioning in a Massachusetts home.

A detail photo reveals the iron works in the fireplace, Massachusetts.

Making pies in the Cooper-Austin house, Massachusetts.

The Hale House parlor, Massachusetts.

"Who will ever be stimulated to improve the appearance of a countryside so long as its edifices are nothing but board boxes?"—W. N.

A parlor in the Concord, Massachusetts, area.

A mirror tops a mantel in a Massachusetts home.

The "middle room" of the Coffin House, Massachusetts

A fireplace in Concord.

The parlor of the Sparhawk home in Kittery.

Parlor scene in Vermont.

A warm parlor in Vermont.

Public Buildings

"Strong and beautiful public buildings will inevitably be followed by dwellings of a better character. A substantial church in good taste will, in process of time, change the architecture of an entire village," Nutting wrote.

The State House in Augusta, Maine.

"Why is it ... that a small dwelling, even a one story cottage of two rooms bowered in trees ... should appeal a thousand times more than a stately dwelling, no matter how beautifully set? ... Here the reason probably lies in the sense of coziness and intimacy with nature which a small dwelling exhibits."—W. N.

A Vermont church, crowned by a double octagonal cupola and spire.

Hubbard Hall on the
Bowdoin College Cam-
pus, Brunswick, Maine.

The Unitarian
Church in Lancaster,
Massachusetts.

125

An old ship church in Hingham, Massachusetts.

The Church of New England, Connecticut.

A four-storey church in Bedford, Massachusetts.

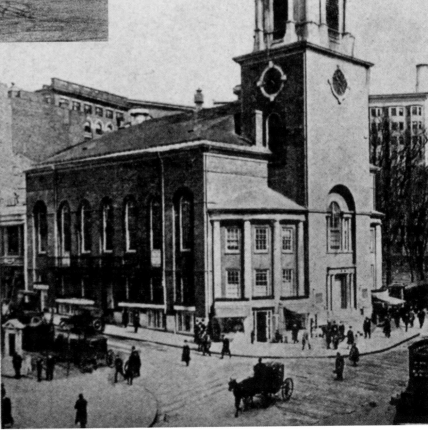

The Park Street Church, Massachusetts.

127

Westmoreland Church, New Hampshire.

Nashua's Civic Center, New Hampshire.

128

Inside St. John's Church, Portsmouth, New Hampshire.

The Old York Jail, Maine.

The entrance to the Wayside Inn, Massachusetts.

"A cottage ... if it still has a stone wall or a post and rail fence about it, or even a picket fence, a few shade trees, and if it stands back somewhat from the street, is a very good example of the sort of home which meets all human need and possibly may be looked forward to as a future possession of every family, even the poorest. Meantime, it appeals to persons of the best taste as a desirable summer residence and by its unpretentious merits and simple beauty is in a way to teach us the quiet life."—W. N.

Parson Capen House in Topsfield, Massachusetts.

The ancient Town Pound in Durham, New Hampshire, was where folks went looking for animals gone astray. In those days, it was more likely valuable livestock than beloved pets they took the time to find.

"A little old school house like this might become a kind of local museum of patriotism, of memory and of sentiment, and might serve to embody for the coming generation the idea of the country school as it was."

A schoolhouse in Westmoreland, New Hamsphire.

An old inn located in Woodstock, Connecticut.

The corner of a common in south Woodstock, Connecticut.

Homes on Old Chestnut Street in Salem.

A Newburyport, Massachusetts, spire.

A residential street in Montpelier, Vermont.

Brookfield center, Connecticut.

A stately residential street in Montpelier, Vermont.

"Oh, Fashion, what crimes are committed in thy name!"—W. N.

A village in Nantucket.

Roof lines of Nantucket.

Broadway, Nantucket.

A commercial scene in East Hartford, Connecticut.

The New England Meeting House in Rockingham, Maine.

The old inn located in Sudbury, Vermont.

Fort Western, Augusta, Maine.

Fort Halifax in Winslow, Maine.

Pemaquid Fort, Maine.

The Old Inn located in North Brookfield, Massachusetts.

Wayside Inn, Massachusetts.

"A fine conservative spirit which desires to retain the old homestead and its furniture, although both are marked by honorable scars, is one of the better aspects of civilization."—W. N.

Fish houses in Great Chebeague, Massachusetts.

The Wayside Inn and garden.

The Middle Haddam Library in Connecticut.

A public building in Colchester, Connecticut.

The Old Rockingham Church, New Hampshire. "The old Rockingham church is remarkable for the great number of lights in the windows and also for its door in the side, which is an early type."

The Cincinnati Chapter, Exeter, New Hampshire.

The Mill, circa 1653, in New London, Connecticut.

"It is far easier to learn the orders of architecture than it is to harmonize one's plan with the region and to place one's home so that it may appear as a part of the landscape."—W. N.

Sergeant Larrabee's Garrison, Kennebunk, 1724.

The old red schoolhouse in Vermont.